ESSENTIAL

Vegetarian

p

Contents

Introduction

People choose to eat vegetarian food for a variety of reasons, whether it be because they care about their health, are concerned about the moral issue of eating meat or simply because they enjoy the flavour of vegetarian food. If you have not tried vegetarian cooking before, you are certain to be converted as the vegetarian diet is not only versatile, but colourful and flavoursome too. An enormous range of natural food and produce is available, so it is hardly surprising that the quality and variety of vegetarian food is so good. Indeed, fresh produce from all over the world is now available in most supermarkets, from lychees, native to South East Asia, to the popular pineapple, native to Central and South America.

The use of fresh fruit, vegetables, herbs and spices means that the vegetarian diet is a healthy one. However, it is important that you ensure your diet is balanced and that you consume adequate quantities of protein. This should not be a problem however as there are plenty of foods to choose from. Eggs, cheese, milk, nuts, beans and soya products are all excellent sources.

Another benefit of the vegetarian diet is that it is rich in vitamins. The best sources of vitamin A are yellow fruits and vegetables. However, it is also present in butter and some green vegetables. Vitamin A keeps the skin, hair, eyes and body tissues in healthy condition and helps prevent infections. The B vitamins act as a catalyst in releasing energy from food and are essential for the maintenance of red blood cells and a healthy nervous system. With the exception of B12 all the B vitamins can be found in yeast and wholegrain cereals. Vegans (who do not eat dairy products) should include a B12 supplement in their diet. Vitamin C can be found in fresh fruit and vegetables and is renowned for preventing infections as well helping to cure winter colds and flu. Eating foods with vitamin C alongside iron-rich foods is recommended, as your body will absorb higher levels of iron than in other circumstances. The last important vitamin is vitamin D, which enables the body to absorb calcium, and therefore helps to make and maintain healthy strong bones and teeth.

Once you have tried vegetarian cooking you will experience just how delicious it is. Be careful however, especially when buying products such as cheese and wine, that the packaging displays the *V* symbol. By following the recipes in this book and by using wonderful vegetarian ingredients you can create and enjoy healthy meat-free meals.

Italian Cream of Tomato Soup

Serves 4

INGREDIENTS

60 g/2 oz/4 tbsp unsalted
    butter
1 large onion, chopped
900 g/2 lb Italian plum
    tomatoes, skinned and
    roughly chopped

600 ml/1 pint/2¹/₂ cups
    vegetable stock
pinch of bicarbonate of soda
    (baking soda)
225 g/8 oz/2 cups dried fusilli
1 tbsp caster (superfine) sugar

150 ml/¹/₄ pint/⁵/₈ cup double
    (heavy) cream
salt and pepper
fresh basil leaves, to garnish
deep-fried croûtons, to serve

1 Melt the butter in a pan and fry the onion until softened. Add the chopped tomatoes, with 300 ml/ ½ pint/1¼ cups of vegetable stock and the bicarbonate of soda (baking soda). Bring the soup to the boil and simmer for 20 minutes.

2 Remove the pan from the heat and set aside to cool. Purée the soup in a blender or food processor and pour through a fine strainer back into the saucepan.

3 Add the remaining vegetable stock and the fusilli to the pan, and season to taste.

4 Add the sugar to the pan, bring to the boil, then simmer for about 15 minutes.

5 Pour the soup into warm soup bowls, swirl the double (heavy) cream around the surface of the soup and garnish with fresh basil leaves. Serve immediately with deep-fried croûtons.

VARIATION

To make orange and tomato soup, simply use half the quantity of vegetable stock, topped up with the same amount of fresh orange juice and garnish the soup with orange rind. Or to make tomato and carrot soup, add half the quantity again of vegetable stock with the same amount of carrot juice and 175 g/6 oz/1¼ cups grated carrot to the recipe, cooking the carrot with the onion.

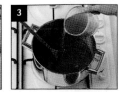

Lentil, Pasta & Vegetable Soup

Serves 4

INGREDIENTS

1 tbsp olive oil
1 medium onion, chopped
4 garlic cloves, finely chopped
350 g/12 oz carrot, sliced
1 stick celery, sliced
225 g/8 oz/1¼ cups red
 lentils

600 ml/1 pint/2½ cups fresh
 vegetable stock
700 ml/1¼ pint/scant 3 cups
 boiling water
150 g/5½ oz/scant 1 cup
 pasta

150 ml/5 fl oz/²/3 cup natural
 low-fat fromage frais
 (unsweetened yogurt)
salt and pepper
2 tbsp fresh parsley, chopped,
 to garnish

1 Heat the oil in a large saucepan and gently fry the prepared onion, garlic, carrot and celery, stirring gently, for 5 minutes until the vegetables begin to soften.

2 Add the lentils, stock and boiling water. Season with salt and pepper to taste, stir and bring back to the boil. Simmer, uncovered, for 15 minutes until the lentils are completely tender. Allow to cool for 10 minutes.

3 Meanwhile, bring another saucepan of water to the boil and cook the pasta according to the instructions on the packet. Drain well and set aside.

4 Place the soup in a blender and process until smooth. Return to a saucepan and add the pasta. Bring back to a simmer and heat for 2–3 minutes until piping hot. Remove from the heat and stir in the fromage frais (yogurt). Season if necessary.

5 Serve sprinkled with chopped parsley.

COOK'S TIP

Avoid boiling the soup once the fromage frais (yogurt) has been added. Otherwise it will separate and become watery, spoiling the appearance of the soup.

Tomato & Red (Bell) Pepper Soup

Serves 4

INGREDIENTS

2 large red (bell) peppers
1 large onion, chopped
2 sticks celery, trimmed and
   chopped
1 garlic clove, crushed

600 ml/1 pint/2^1/$_2$ cups fresh
   vegetable stock
2 bay leaves
2 x 400 g/14 oz cans plum
   tomatoes

salt and pepper
2 spring onions (scallions),
   finely shredded, to garnish
crusty bread, to serve

1 Preheat the grill (broiler) to hot. Halve and deseed the (bell) peppers, arrange them on the grill (broiler) rack and cook, turning occasionally, for 8–10 minutes until softened and charred.

2 Leave to cool slightly, then carefully peel off the charred skin. Reserving a small piece for garnish, chop the (bell) pepper flesh and place in a large saucepan.

3 Mix in the onion, celery and garlic. Add the stock and the bay leaves. Bring to the boil, cover and simmer for 15 minutes. Remove from the heat.

4 Stir in the tomatoes and transfer to a blender. Process for a few seconds until smooth. Return to the saucepan.

5 Season to taste and heat for 3–4 minutes until piping hot. Ladle into warm bowls and garnish with the reserved (bell) pepper cut into strips and the spring onion (scallion). Serve with crusty bread.

COOK'S TIP

If you prefer a coarser, more robust soup, lightly mash the tomatoes with a wooden spoon and omit the blending process in step 4.

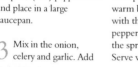

Carrot, Apple & Celery Soup

Serves 4

INGREDIENTS

900 g/2 lb carrots, finely diced
1 medium onion, chopped
3 sticks celery, diced
1 litre/1³/₄ pints/1 quart fresh
   vegetable stock

3 medium-sized eating
   (dessert) apples
2 tbsp tomato purée (paste)
1 bay leaf
2 tsp caster (superfine) sugar

¹/₄ large lemon
salt and pepper
celery leaves, washed and
   shredded, to garnish

1 Place the carrots, onion and celery in a large saucepan and add the stock. Bring to the boil, cover and simmer for 10 minutes.

2 Meanwhile, peel, core and dice 2 of the eating (dessert) apples. Add the pieces of apple, tomato purée (paste), bay leaf and caster (superfine) sugar to the saucepan and bring to the boil. Reduce the heat, half cover and allow to simmer for 20 minutes. Remove and discard the bay leaf.

3 Meanwhile, wash, core and cut the remaining apple into thin slices, leaving on the skin. Place the apple slices in a small saucepan and squeeze over the lemon juice. Heat gently and simmer for 1–2 minutes until tender. Drain and set aside.

4 Place the carrot and apple mixture in a blender or food processor and blend until smooth. Alternatively, press the carrot and apple mixture through a sieve with the back of a wooden spoon.

5 Gently re-heat the soup if necessary and season with salt and pepper to taste. Ladle the soup into warm bowls and serve topped with the reserved apple slices and shredded celery leaves.

COOK'S TIP

Soaking light coloured fruit in lemon juice helps to prevent it from turning brown.

Rosy Melon & Strawberries

Serves 4

INGREDIENTS

1/4 honeydew melon	150 ml/5 fl oz/2/3 cup rosé	175 g/6 oz small strawberries,
1/2 Charentais or Cantaloupe	wine	washed and hulled
melon	2–3 tsp rose water	rose petals, to garnish

1 Scoop out the seeds from both melons with a spoon. Then carefully remove the skin, taking care not to remove too much flesh.

2 Cut the melon flesh into thin strips and place in a bowl. Pour over the wine and sufficient rose water to taste. Mix together gently, cover and leave to chill in the refrigerator for at least 2 hours.

3 Halve the strawberries and carefully mix into the melon. Allow the melon and strawberries to stand at room temperature for about 15 minutes for the flavours to develop – if the melon is too cold, there will be little flavour.

4 Arrange on individual serving plates and serve sprinkled with a few rose petals, if wished.

COOK'S TIP

Rose water is a distillation of rose petals. It is generally available from large pharmacies and leading supermarkets as well as from more specialist food suppliers.

VARIATION

It does not matter whether the rosé wine is sweet or dry – although sweet wine contains more calories. Experiment with different types of melon. Varieties such as 'Sweet Dream' have whitish-green flesh, while Charentais melons, which have orange flesh, are fragrant and go better with a dry wine. If you wish, soak the strawberries in the wine with the melon, but always allow the fruit to return to room temperature before serving.

Colourful Vegetable Kebabs (Kabobs)

Serves 4

INGREDIENTS

1 red (bell) pepper, deseeded	1 small onion	SEASONED OIL:
1 yellow (bell) pepper, deseeded	8 cherry tomatoes	6 tbsp olive oil
1 green (bell) pepper, deseeded	100 g/3¹/₂ oz wild mushrooms	1 clove garlic, crushed
		¹/₂ tsp mixed dried herbs or herbes de Provence

1 Cut the (bell) peppers into 2.5 cm/1 inch pieces.

2 Peel the onion and cut it into wedges, leaving the root end just intact to help keep the wedges together.

3 Thread the (bell) peppers, onion wedges, tomatoes and mushrooms on to skewers, alternating the colours of the (bell) peppers.

4 To make the seasoned oil, mix together the oil, garlic and herbs in a small bowl. Brush the mixture liberally over the kebabs (kabobs).

5 Barbecue (grill) the kebabs (kabobs) over medium hot coals for 10–15 minutes, brushing with more of the seasoned oil and turning the skewers frequently.

6 Transfer the vegetable kebabs (kabobs) to warm serving plates. Serve the kebabs (kabobs) with walnut sauce (see Cook's Tip, right), if you wish.

COOK'S TIP

These kebabs (kabobs) are delicious when accompanied with a walnut sauce. To make the sauce, process 125 g/4 ¹/₂ oz walnuts in a food processor until they form a smooth paste. With the machine running, add 150 ml/5 fl oz/²/₃ cup double (heavy) cream and 1 tablespoon of olive oil. Season to taste. Alternatively, finely chop the walnuts then pound them in a pestle and mortar to form a paste. Mix with the cream and oil, and season.

Nutty Rice Burgers

Makes 6

INGREDIENTS

1 tbsp sunflower oil
1 small onion, chopped finely
100 g/3^1/2 oz mushrooms,
   chopped finely
350 g/12 oz/8 cups cooked
   brown rice
100 g/3^1/2 oz breadcrumbs
75 g/2^3/4 oz walnuts, chopped

1 egg
2 tbsp brown fruity sauce
dash of Tabasco sauce
salt and pepper
oil, to baste
6 individual cheese slices
   (optional)

TO SERVE:
6 sesame seed baps
slices of onion
slices of tomato
green salad leaves

1 Heat the oil in a pan and fry the onions for 3–4 minutes until they just begin to soften. Add the mushrooms and cook for a further 2 minutes.

2 Remove the pan from the heat and mix the rice, breadcrumbs, walnuts, egg and sauces into the vegetables. Season with salt and pepper and mix well.

3 Shape the mixture into 6 burgers, pressing the mixture together with your fingers. Leave to chill in the refrigerator for at least 30 minutes.

4 Barbecue (grill) the burgers on an oiled rack over medium coals for 5–6 minutes on each side, turning once and frequently basting with oil.

5 If liked, top the burgers with a slice of cheese 2 minutes before the end of the cooking time. Barbecue (grill) the onion and tomato slices.

6 Toast the sesame seed baps at the side of the barbecue. Serve the burgers in the baps, together with the barbecued (grilled) onions and tomatoes.

Stuffed Tomatoes

Makes 8

INGREDIENTS

4 beefsteak tomatoes
300 g/10^1/2 oz/4^1/2 cups
    cooked rice
8 spring onions (scallions),
    chopped

3 tbsp chopped, fresh mint
2 tbsp chopped, fresh parsley
3 tbsp pine nuts
3 tbsp raisins
2 tsp olive oil

salt and pepper

1 Cut the tomatoes in half, then scoop out the seeds and discard.

2 Stand the tomatoes upside down on absorbent kitchen paper for a few moments in order for the juices to drain out.

3 Turn the tomatoes the right way up and sprinkle the insides with salt and pepper.

4 Mix together the rice, spring onions (scallions), mint, parsley, pine nuts and raisins.

Spoon the mixture into the tomato cups.

5 Drizzle over a little olive oil, then barbecue (grill) the tomatoes on an oiled rack over medium hot coals for about 10 minutes until they are tender.

6 Transfer the tomatoes to serving plates and serve immediately.

COOK'S TIP

Tomatoes are a popular barbecue (grill) vegetable and can be quickly cooked. Try grilling (broiling) slices of beefsteak tomato and slices of onion brushed with a little oil and topped with sprigs of fresh herbs. In addition, cherry tomatoes can be threaded on to skewers and barbecued (grilled) for 5–10 minutes until hot.

Fragrant Asparagus & Orange Risotto

Serves 4–6

INGREDIENTS

115 g/4 oz fine asparagus
    spears, trimmed
1.2 litres/2 pints/5 cups
    vegetable stock
2 bulbs fennel
25 g/1 oz low-fat spread

1 tsp olive oil
2 sticks celery, trimmed and
    chopped
2 medium leeks, trimmed
    and shredded

350 g/12 oz/2 cups arborio
    rice
3 medium oranges
salt and pepper

1 Bring a small saucepan of water to the boil and cook the asparagus for 1 minute. Drain and set aside until required.

2 Pour the stock into a saucepan and bring to the boil. Reduce the heat to maintain a gentle simmer.

3 Meanwhile, trim the fennel, reserving the fronds, and cut into thin slices. Carefully melt the low-fat spread with the oil in a large saucepan, taking care that the water in the low-fat spread does not evaporate, and gently fry the fennel, celery and leeks for 3–4 minutes until just softened. Add the rice and cook, stirring, for a further 2 minutes until mixed.

4 Add a ladleful of stock to the pan and cook gently, stirring, until absorbed. Continue ladling the stock into the rice until the rice becomes creamy, thick and tender. This process will take about 25 minutes and shouldn't be hurried.

5 Finely grate the rind and extract the juice from 1 orange and mix in to the rice. Carefully remove the peel and pith from the remaining oranges. Holding the fruit over the saucepan, cut out the orange segments and add to the rice, along with any juice that falls.

6 Stir the orange into the rice along with the asparagus spears. Season with salt and pepper, garnish with the reserved fennel fronds, and serve.

Pear & Roquefort Salad

Serves 4

INGREDIENTS

50 g/1³/4 oz Roquefort cheese
150 ml/5 fl oz/²/3 cup low-fat
    natural yogurt
2 tbsp snipped chives

few leaves of lollo rosso
few leaves of radiccio
few leaves of lamb's lettuce
    (corn salad)

2 ripe pears
pepper
whole chives, to garnish

1 Place the cheese in a bowl and mash with a fork. Gradually blend the yogurt into the cheese to make a smooth dressing. Add the chives and season with a little pepper according to taste.

2 Tear the lollo rosso, radiccio and lamb's lettuce leaves into manageable pieces. Arrange the salad leaves on a serving platter or on individual serving plates.

3 Quarter and core the pears and then cut them into slices.

4 Arrange the pear slices over the salad leaves.

5 Drizzle the dressing over the pears and garnish with a few whole chives. Serve at once.

COOK'S TIP

Arrange the Pear and Roquefort Salad on individual plates for an attractive starter, or on one large serving platter for a side salad.

COOK'S TIP

Look out for bags of mixed salad leaves as these are generally more economical than buying lots of different leaves separately. If you are using leaves that have not been prewashed, rinse them well and dry them thoroughly on absorbent paper kitchen towels or in a salad spinner. Alternatively, wrap the leaves in a clean tea towel (dish cloth) and shake dry.

Tabouleh

Serves 4

INGREDIENTS

225 g/8 oz/2 cups cracked
wheat
225 g/8 oz tomatoes
1 small onion
$^1/_4$ cucumber

$^1/_2$ red (bell) pepper
4 tbsp chopped, fresh parsley
3 tbsp chopped, fresh mint
2 tbsp pine nuts
4 tbsp lemon juice

4 tbsp extra virgin olive oil
2 cloves garlic, crushed
salt and pepper

1 Place the cracked wheat in a large bowl and cover with plenty of boiling water. Leave to stand for about 30 minutes or until the grains are tender and have swelled in size.

2 Drain the wheat through a large sieve. Press down with a plate in order to remove as much water as possible. Transfer the wheat to a large bowl.

3 Cut the tomatoes in half, scoop out the seeds and discard them. Chop the flesh into fine

dice. Using a sharp knife, finely chop the onion.

4 Scoop out the seeds from the cucumber and discard them. Finely dice the cucumber flesh.

5 Deseed the (bell) peppers and chop the flesh. Add the prepared vegetables to the wheat with the herbs and pine nuts. Toss until mixed.

6 Mix together the lemon juice oil, garlic and salt and pepper to taste in a small bowl.

7 Pour the mixture over the wheat and vegetables and toss together. Leave to chill in the refrigerator until required.

COOK'S TIP

This salad is best made a few hours before it is required to allow time for the flavours to develop and blend together. It can even be made a few days ahead, if wished.

Soft Pancakes with Stir-fried Vegetables & Tofu (Bean Curd)

Serves 4

INGREDIENTS

1 tbsp vegetable oil
1 garlic clove, crushed
2.5 cm/1 inch piece root
  (fresh) ginger, grated
1 bunch spring onions
  (scallions), trimmed and
  shredded lengthwise
100 g/3^1/2 oz mangetout
  (snow peas), topped, tailed
  and shredded

225 g/8 oz tofu (bean curd),
  drained and cut into
  1 cm/^{1}/2 inch pieces
2 tbsp dark soy sauce, plus
  extra to serve
2 tbsp hoi-sin sauce, plus
  extra to serve
60 g/2 oz canned bamboo
  shoots, drained
60 g/2 oz canned water
  chestnuts, drained and
  sliced

100 g/3^1/2 oz bean sprouts
1 small red chilli, deseeded
  and sliced thinly
1 small bunch fresh chives
12 soft Chinese pancakes

TO SERVE:
shredded Chinese leaves
1 cucumber, sliced
strips of red chilli

1 Heat the oil in a non-stick wok or a large frying pan (skillet) and stir-fry the garlic and ginger for 1 minute. Add the spring onions (scallions), mangetout (snow peas), tofu (bean curd), soy and hoi-sin sauces. Stir-fry for 2 minutes.

2 Add the bamboo shoots, water chestnuts, bean sprouts and red chilli to the pan. Stir-fry for 2 minutes until the vegetables are tender but still have bite. Snip the chives into 2.5 cm/1 inch lengths and stir them into the mixture in the pan.

3 Heat the pancakes according to the instructions on the packet and keep warm.

4 Divide the vegetables and tofu (bean curd) among the pancakes. Roll up the pancakes and serve with the Chinese leaves.

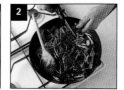

Spicy Black-Eyed Beans

Serves 4

INGREDIENTS

350 g/12 oz/2 cups black-eyed
   beans, soaked overnight in
   cold water
1 tbsp vegetable oil
2 medium onions, chopped
1 tbsp clear honey
2 tbsp treacle (molasses)
4 tbsp dark soy sauce

1 tsp dry mustard powder
4 tbsp tomato purée (paste)
450 ml/16 fl oz/2 cups fresh
   vegetable stock
1 bay leaf
1 sprig each of rosemary,
   thyme and sage
1 small orange

1 tbsp cornflour (cornstarch)
2 medium red (bell) peppers,
   deseeded and diced
pepper
2 tbsp chopped fresh flat-leaf
   parsley, to garnish
crusty bread, to serve

1 Preheat the oven to 150°C/300°F/Gas Mark 2. Rinse the beans and place in a saucepan. Cover with water, bring to the boil and boil rapidly for 10 minutes. Drain and place in an ovenproof casserole dish.

2 Meanwhile, heat the oil in a frying pan (skillet) and fry the onions for 5 minutes. Stir in the honey, treacle (molasses), soy sauce, mustard and tomato purée (paste). Pour in the stock, bring to the boil and pour the mixture over the beans.

3 Tie the bay leaf, rosemary, thyme and sage together with a clean piece of string and add to the pan containing the beans. Using a vegetable peeler, pare off 3 pieces of orange rind and mix into the beans, along with plenty of pepper. Cover and bake for 1 hour.

4 Extract the juice from the orange and blend with the cornflour (cornstarch) to form a paste. Stir into the beans along with the red (bell) peppers. Cover and cook for 1 hour, until the sauce is rich and thick and the beans are tender. Discard the herbs and orange rind.

5 Garnish with chopped fresh flat-leaf parsley and serve with fresh crusty bread.

Aubergines (Eggplants) & Yogurt

Serves 4

INGREDIENTS

2 medium aubergines
   (eggplants)
4 tbsp oil
1 medium onion, sliced

1 tsp white cumin seeds
1 tsp chilli powder
1 tsp salt

3 tbsp natural yogurt
1/2 tsp mint sauce
chopped mint leaves, to
   garnish

1 Rinse the aubergines (eggplants) and pat dry with paper towels.

2 Place the aubergines (eggplants) in an ovenproof dish. Bake in a pre-heated oven, 160°C/425°F/Gas Mark 3, for 45 minutes. Remove the baked aubergines (eggplants) from the oven and leave to cool.

3 Slice each aubergine (eggplant) in half with a sharp knife and, using a spoon, scoop out the aubergine (eggplant) flesh and reserve.

4 Heat the oil in a heavy-based saucepan. Add the onions and cumin seeds and fry, stirring constantly, for 1-2 minutes.

5 Add the chilli powder, salt, natural yogurt and the mint sauce to the saucepan and stir the mixture well to combine.

6 Add the aubergine (eggplant) flesh to the onion and yogurt mixture in the pan and stir-fry for 5-7 minutes or until all of the liquid has been absorbed and the mixture is quite dry.

7 Transfer the aubergine (eggplant) and yogurt mixture to a serving dish and garnish with chopped mint leaves.

COOK'S TIP

Rich in protein and calcium, yogurt plays an important part in Indian cooking. Thick natural yogurt most closely resembles the yogurt made in many Indian homes.

Spinach & Cheese Curry

Serves 4

INGREDIENTS

300 ml/^{1}/$_2$ pint/1^1/$_4$ cups oil
200 g/7 oz panir, cubed (see
   Cook's Tip)

3 tomatoes, sliced
1 tsp ground cumin
1^1/$_2$ tsp ground chilli powder

1 tsp salt
400 g/14 oz spinach
3 green chillies

1 Heat the oil in a large frying pan (skillet). Add the cubed panir and fry, stirring occasionally, until golden brown.

2 Remove the panir from the frying pan (skillet) with a perforated spoon and leave to drain on kitchen paper.

3 Add the tomatoes to the remaining oil in the pan and stir-fry, breaking up the tomatoes, for 5 minutes.

4 Add the ground cumin, chilli powder and salt and mix well.

5 Add the spinach to the pan and stir-fry over a low heat for 7-10 minutes.

6 Add the green chillies and the panir and cook, stirring, for a further 2 minutes.

7 Transfer the curry to serving plates and serve hot with pooris or plain boiled rice.

VARIATION

You could used frozen spinach in this recipe. It should be thawed and squeezed dry before using.

COOK'S TIP

To make panir, boil 1 litre/ 1^3/$_4$ pints/4^1/$_2$ cups milk slowly over a low heat, then add 2 tbsp lemon juice, stirring continuously and gently until the milk thickens and begins to curdle. Strain the curdled milk through a sieve. Set aside under a heavy weight for about 1^1/$_2$-2 hours to press to a flat shape about 1 cm/^{1}/$_2$ inch thick. Once set, the panir can be cut, like cheese, into whatever shape is required.

Vegetable Curry

Serves 4

INGREDIENTS

250 g/8 oz turnips or swede, peeled
1 aubergine (eggplant), leaf end trimmed
350 g/12 oz new potatoes, scrubbed
250 g/8 oz cauliflower
250 g/8 oz button mushrooms
1 large onion
250 g/8 oz carrots, peeled
6 tbsp vegetable ghee or oil

2 garlic cloves, crushed
5 cm/2 inch ginger root, chopped finely
1-2 fresh green chillies, seeded and chopped
1 tbsp paprika
2 tsp ground coriander
1 tbsp mild or medium curry powder or paste
450 ml/³/4 pint/1³/4 cups vegetable stock

400 g/14 oz can chopped tomatoes
1 green (bell) pepper, seeded and sliced
1 tbsp cornflour (cornstarch)
150 ml/¹/4 pint/²/3 cup coconut milk
2-3 tbsp ground almonds
salt
fresh coriander (cilantro) sprigs, to garnish

1 Cut the turnips or swede, aubergine (eggplant) and potatoes into 1 cm/¹/2 inch cubes. Divide the cauliflower into small florets. Leave the mushrooms whole and slice the onion and carrots.

2 Heat the ghee or oil in a large saucepan, add the onion, turnip, potato and cauliflower and cook

gently for 3 minutes, stirring frequently. Add the garlic, ginger, chillies, paprika, ground coriander and curry powder or paste and cook for 1 minute.

3 Add the stock, tomatoes, aubergine (eggplant) and mushrooms and season with salt. Cover and simmer for 30 minutes or until tender. Add the

(bell) pepper and carrots, cover and cook for a further 5 minutes.

4 Blend the cornflour (cornstarch) with the coconut milk and stir into the mixture. Add ground almonds and simmer for 2 minutes, stirring all the time. Transfer to serving plates and garnish with fresh coriander (cilantro).

Dumplings in Yogurt Sauce

Serves 4

INGREDIENTS

DUMPLINGS:
100 g/3^1/2 oz/^{3}/4 cup gram flour
1 tsp chilli powder
^{1}/2 tsp salt
^{1}/2 tsp bicarbonate of soda (baking soda)
1 medium onion, finely chopped
2 green chillies
fresh coriander (cilantro)

150 ml/^{1}/4 pint/^{2}/3 cup water
300 ml/^{1}/2 pint/1^1/4 cups oil

YOGURT SAUCE:
300 ml/^{1}/2 pint/1^1/4 cups yogurt
3 tbsp gram flour
150 ml/^{1}/4 pint/^{2}/3 cup water
1 tsp fresh ginger root, chopped
1 tsp fresh garlic, crushed

1^1/2 tsp chilli powder
1^1/2 tsp salt
^{1}/2 tsp turmeric
1 tsp ground coriander
5 ml/1 tsp ground cumin

SEASONED DRESSING:
150 ml/^{1}/4 pint/^{2}/3 cup oil
1 tsp white cumin seeds
6 red dried chillies

1 To make the dumplings, sieve the gram flour into a large bowl. Add the chilli powder, salt, soda, onion, green chillies and coriander (cilantro) and mix. Add the water and mix to form a thick paste. Heat the oil in a frying-pan (skillet). Drop teaspoonfuls of the paste in the oil and fry over a medium heat, until golden.

2 To make the sauce, place the yogurt in a bowl and whisk with the gram flour and the water. Add all of the spices and garlic, and mix well. Push this mixture through a large sieve into a saucepan. Bring the sauce to a boil over a low heat while stirring continuously. If the yogurt sauce becomes too thick add a little extra water.

3 Pour the sauce into a deep serving dish and arrange the dumplings on top. Keep warm.

4 To make the dressing, heat the oil in a frying-pan (skillet). Add the white cumin seeds and the dried red chillies and fry until darker in colour. Pour the dressing over the dumplings and serve hot.

Courgettes (Zucchini) & Fenugreek Seeds

Serves 4

INGREDIENTS

6 tbsp oil	chopped finely	2 tomatoes, sliced
1 medium onion, finely	1 tsp fresh garlic, crushed	fresh coriander (cilantro)
chopped	1 tsp chilli powder	leaves, plus extra to
3 green chillies, finely chopped	450 g/1 lb courgettes	garnish
1 tsp fresh ginger root,	(zucchini), sliced	2 tsp fenugreek seeds

1 Heat the oil in a large frying pan (skillet).

2 Add the onion, green chillies, ginger, garlic and chilli powder to the pan, stirring well to combine.

3 Add the sliced courgettes (zucchini) and the sliced tomatoes to the pan and stir-fry for 5–7 minutes.

4 Add the cilantro (coriander) and fenugreek seeds to the courgette (zucchini) mixture in the pan and stir-fry for 5 minutes.

5 Remove the pan from the heat and transfer the courgette (zucchini) and fenugreek seed mixture to serving dishes. Garnish and serve hot with Chapatis.

COOK'S TIP

Both the leaves and seeds of fenugreek are used, but the stalks and root should be discarded, as they have a bitter taste. Fresh fenugreek is sold in bunches. Fenugreek seeds are flat and yellowish brown in colour. You could use coriander seeds instead of the fenugreek seeds, if you prefer.

Green Bean & Potato Curry

Serves 4

INGREDIENTS

300 ml/$\frac{1}{2}$ pint/1$\frac{1}{4}$ cups oil
1 tsp white cumin seeds
1 tsp mustard and onion seeds
4 dried red chillies
3 fresh tomatoes, sliced
1 tsp salt

1 tsp fresh ginger root, finely chopped
1 tsp fresh garlic, crushed
1 tsp chilli powder
200 g/7 oz green cut beans
2 medium potatoes, peeled and diced

300 ml/$\frac{1}{2}$ pint/1$\frac{1}{4}$ cups water
fresh coriander (cilantro) leaves, chopped
2 green chillies, finely chopped

1 Heat the oil in a large, heavy-based saucepan.

2 Add the white cumin seeds, mustard and onion seeds and dried red chillies to the saucepan, stirring well.

3 Add the tomato slices to the saucepan and stir-fry the mixture for 3-5 minutes.

4 Mix together the salt, ginger, garlic and chilli powder and spoon into the pan. Blend the whole mixture together.

5 Add the green beans and potatoes to the pan and stir-fry for about 5 minutes.

6 Add the water to the pan, reduce the heat and leave to simmer for 10-15 minutes, stirring occasionally.

7 Garnish the green bean and potato curry with chopped coriander (cilantro) leaves and green chillies and serve hot with cooked rice.

COOK'S TIP

Mustard seeds are often fried in oil or ghee to bring out their flavour before being combined with other ingredients.

Tofu (Bean Curd) Casserole

Serves 4

INGREDIENTS

450 g/1 lb tofu (bean curd)
2 tbsp peanut oil
8 spring onions (scallions), cut
 into batons
2 celery sticks, sliced
125 g/4¹/2 oz broccoli florets
125 g/4¹/2 oz courgettes
 (zucchini), sliced

2 garlic cloves, thinly sliced
450 g/1 lb baby spinach
rice, to serve

SAUCE:
425 ml/³/4 pint/2 cups
 vegetable stock
2 tbsp light soy sauce

3 tbsp hoisin sauce
¹/2 tsp chilli powder
1 tbsp sesame oil

1 Cut the tofu (bean curd) into 2.5-cm/1-inch cubes and set aside.

2 Heat the oil in a preheated wok. Add the spring onions (scallions), celery, broccoli, courgettes (zucchini), garlic, spinach and tofu (bean curd) and stir-fry for 3–4 minutes.

3 To make the sauce, mix together the vegetable stock, soy sauce, hoisin sauce, chilli powder and sesame oil in a flameproof casserole and bring to the boil. Add the vegetables and tofu (bean curd), reduce the heat, cover and simmer for 10 minutes.

4 Transfer to a warm serving dish and serve with rice.

COOK'S TIP

This recipe has a green vegetable theme, but alter the colour and flavour by adding your favourite vegetables, if you prefer.

VARIATION

Add 75 g/3 oz fresh or canned and drained straw mushrooms with the vegetables in step 2.

Spicy Vegetarian Fried Triangles

Serves 4

INGREDIENTS

1 tbsp sea salt	2 garlic cloves, crushed	vegetable oil, for deep-frying
4 1/2 tsp Chinese five spice powder	1 tsp grated fresh root ginger	2 leeks, halved and shredded
3 tbsp light brown sugar	2 x 225 g/8 oz cakes tofu (bean curd)	shredded leek, to garnish

1 Mix the salt, Chinese five spice, sugar, garlic and ginger in a bowl and transfer to a plate.

2 Cut the tofu (bean curd) cakes in half diagonally to form two triangles. Cut each triangle in half and then in half again to form 16 triangles.

3 Roll the tofu (bean curd) triangles in the spice mixture, turning to coat thoroughly. Set aside for 1 hour.

4 Heat the oil for deep-frying in a wok until it is almost smoking. Reduce the heat slightly, add the tofu (bean curd) triangles and fry for 5 minutes, until golden brown. Remove from the wok with a slotted spoon and set aside.

5 Add the leeks to the wok and stir-fry for 1 minute. Remove from the wok with a slotted spoon and drain on absorbent kitchen paper (paper towels).

6 Arrange the leeks on a warm serving plate and place the fried tofu (bean curd) on top. Garnish with the fresh shredded leek and serve immediately.

COOK'S TIP

Fry the tofu (bean curd) in batches and keep each batch warm until all of the tofu (bean curd) has been fried and is ready to serve.

Gingered Broccoli

Serves 4

INGREDIENTS

2 tbsp peanut oil
1 garlic clove, crushed
5-cm/2-inch piece fresh root
    ginger, finely chopped
675 g/1^1/2 lb broccoli florets

1 leek, sliced
75 g/2^3/4 oz water chestnuts,
    halved
^{1}/2 tsp caster (superfine) sugar

125 ml/4 fl oz/^{1}/2 cup
    vegetable stock
1 tsp dark soy sauce
1 tsp cornflour (cornstarch)
2 tsp water

1 Heat the oil in a preheated wok. Add the garlic and ginger and stir-fry for 30 seconds. Add the broccoli, leek and water chestnuts and stir-fry for a further 3–4 minutes.

2 Add the sugar, stock and soy sauce, reduce the heat and simmer for 4–5 minutes, or until the broccoli is almost cooked.

3 Blend the cornflour (cornstarch) with the water to form a smooth paste and stir it into the wok. Bring to the boil and cook, stirring constantly, for 1 minute. Transfer to a serving dish and serve immediately.

COOK'S TIP

If you prefer a slightly milder ginger flavour, cut the ginger into larger strips, stir-fry as described and then remove from the wok and discard.

VARIATION

You could substitute spinach for the broccoli, if you prefer. Trim the woody ends and cut the remainder into 5-cm/2-inch lengths, keeping the stalks and leaves separate. Add the stalks with the leek in step 1 and add the leafy parts 2 minutes later. Reduce the cooking time in step 2 to 3–4 minutes.

Vegetable Chop Suey

Serves 4

INGREDIENTS

1 yellow (bell) pepper, seeded	60 g/2 oz mangetout (snow	2 tbsp light soy sauce
1 red (bell) pepper, seeded	peas)	125 ml/4 fl oz/$1/2$ cup
1 carrot	2 tbsp peanut oil	vegetable stock
1 courgette (zucchini)	3 garlic cloves, crushed	
1 fennel bulb	1 tsp grated fresh root ginger	
1 onion	125 g/$4^1/2$ oz beansprouts	
	2 tsp light brown sugar	

1 Cut the (bell) peppers, carrot, courgette (zucchini) and fennel into thin slices. Cut the onion into quarters and then cut each quarter in half. Slice the mangetout (snow peas) diagonally to create the maximum surface area.

2 Heat the oil in a preheated wok until it is almost smoking. Add the garlic and ginger and stir-fry for 30 seconds. Add the onion and stir-fry for a further 30 seconds.

3 Add the (bell) peppers, carrot, courgette (zucchini), fennel and mangetout (snow peas) and stir-fry for 2 minutes.

4 Add the beansprouts to the wok and stir in the sugar, soy sauce and stock. Reduce the heat and simmer for 1–2 minutes, until the vegetables are tender and coated in the sauce.

5 Transfer the vegetables and sauce to a serving dish and serve immediately.

COOK'S TIP

Use any combination of colourful vegetables that you have to hand to make this versatile dish.

Corn-on-the-cob

Serves 4

INGREDIENTS

4 cobs of sweetcorn, with husks	1 tbsp chopped, fresh parsley	rind of 1 lemon, grated
100 g/3^1/2 oz butter	1 tsp chopped, fresh chives	salt and pepper
	1 tsp chopped, fresh thyme	

1 To prepare the cobs of sweetcorn, peel back the husks and remove the silken hairs.

2 Fold back the husks and secure them in place with string if necessary.

3 Blanch the cobs of sweetcorn in a large pan of boiling water for about 5 minutes. Remove the cobs with a perforated spoon and drain.

4 Barbecue (grill) the cobs over medium hot coals for 20–30 minutes, turning frequently.

5 Meanwhile, soften the butter and beat in the parsley, chives, thyme, lemon rind and salt and pepper to taste.

6 Transfer the cobs of sweetcorn to serving plates, remove the string and pull back the husks. Serve with a generous portion of herb butter.

COOK'S TIP

When you are buying fresh sweetcorn, look for plump, tightly packed kernels. If you are unable to get fresh cobs, cook frozen sweetcorn cobs on the barbecue (grill). Spread some of the herb butter on to a sheet of double thickness kitchen foil. Wrap the cobs in the foil and barbecue (grill) among the coals for 20–30 minutes.

Spicy Sweet Potato Slices

Serves 4

INGREDIENTS

450 g/1 lb sweet potatoes
2 tbsp sunflower oil

1 tsp chilli sauce
salt and pepper

1 Bring a large pan of water to the boil, add the sweet potatoes and par-boil them for 10 minutes. Drain thoroughly and transfer to a chopping board.

2 Peel the potatoes and cut them into thick slices.

3 Mix together the oil, chilli sauce and salt and pepper to taste in a small bowl.

4 Brush the spicy mixture liberally over one side of the potatoes. Place the potatoes, oil side down, over medium hot coals and barbecue (grill) for 5–6 minutes.

5 Lightly brush the tops of the potatoes with the oil, turn them over and barbecue (grill) for a further 5 minutes or until crisp and golden. Transfer the potatoes to a warm serving dish and serve.

COOK'S TIP

Although it is a vegetable the sweet potato is used in both sweet and savoury dishes. It is very versatile and can be boiled, roasted, fried, or cooked as here over a barbecue (grill).

VARIATION

For a simple spicy dip combine 150 ml/5 fl oz/ 2/3 cup sour cream with 1/2 teaspoon of sugar, 1/2 teaspoon of Dijon mustard and salt and pepper to taste. Leave to chill until required.

Vegetarian Sausages

Makes 8

INGREDIENTS

1 tbsp sunflower oil
1 small onion, chopped finely
50 g/1³/4 oz mushrooms,
    chopped finely
¹/2 red (bell) pepper, deseeded
    and chopped finely

400 g/14 oz can cannellini
    beans, rinsed and drained
100 g/3¹/2 oz fresh
    breadcrumbs
100 g/3¹/2 oz Cheddar cheese,
    grated
1 tsp dried mixed herbs

1 egg yolk
seasoned plain (all-purpose)
    flour
oil, to baste
bread rolls, slices of fried
    onion and tomato relish,
    to serve

1 Heat the oil in a
saucepan and fry the
prepared onion,
mushrooms and (bell)
peppers until softened.

2 Mash the cannellini
beans in a large mixing
bowl. Add the onion,
mushroom and (bell)
pepper mixture, the
breadcrumbs, cheese, herbs
and egg yolk, and mix
together well.

3 Press the mixture
together with your

fingers and shape into
8 sausages.

4 Roll each sausage in
the seasoned flour.
Chill for 30 minutes.

5 Barbecue (grill) the
sausages on a sheet of
oiled foil set over medium
coals for 15–20 minutes,
turning and basting
frequently with oil, until
golden.

6 Split a bread roll down
the middle and insert a

layer of fried onions. Place
the sausage in the roll and
serve with tomato relish.

COOK'S TIP

*Take care not to break the
sausages when you turn
them over. If you have a
hinged rack, oil this and
place the sausages inside,
turning and oiling
frequently.*

Aubergine (Eggplant) & Mozzarella Sandwiches

Serves 2

INGREDIENTS
---

1 large aubergine (eggplant)	2 sun-dried tomatoes,	TO SERVE:
1 tbsp lemon juice	chopped	Italian bread
3 tbsp olive oil	salt and pepper	mixed salad leaves
125 g/4 1/2 oz grated		slices of tomato
Mozzarella cheese		

1 Slice the aubergine (eggplant) into thin rounds.

2 Combine the lemon juice and oil in a bowl and season the mixture with salt and pepper.

3 Brush the aubergine (eggplant) slices with the oil and lemon juice mixture and barbecue (grill) over medium hot coals for 2–3 minutes, without turning, until they are golden on the under side.

4 Turn half of the aubergine (eggplant) slices over and sprinkle with cheese and chopped sun-dried tomatoes.

5 Place the remaining aubergine (eggplant) slices on top of the cheese and tomatoes, turning them so that the cooked side is uppermost.

6 Barbecue (grill) for 1–2 minutes, then carefully turn the sandwich over and barbecue (grill) for 1–2 minutes. Baste with the oil mixture.

7 Serve with Italian bread, mixed salad leaves and tomato.

VARIATION

Try Feta cheese instead of Mozzarella but omit the salt from the basting oil. A creamy goat's cheese would be equally delicious.

Mediterranean Spaghetti

Serves 4

INGREDIENTS

2 tbsp olive oil
1 large, red onion, chopped
2 garlic cloves, crushed
1 tbsp lemon juice
4 baby aubergines (eggplants),
    quartered

600 ml/1 pint/2½ cups
    passata (sieved tomatoes)
2 tsp caster (superfine) sugar
2 tbsp tomato purée (paste)
400 g/14 oz can artichoke
    hearts, drained and halved

115 g/4 oz/1 cup stoned
    (pitted) black olives
350 g/12 oz dried spaghetti
25 g/1 oz/2 tbsp butter
salt and pepper
fresh basil sprigs, to garnish
olive bread, to serve

1 Heat 1 tbsp of the olive oil in a large frying pan (skillet). Add the onion, garlic, lemon juice and aubergines (eggplants) and cook over a low heat for 4–5 minutes, until the onion and aubergines (eggplants) are lightly golden brown.

2 Pour in the passata (sieved tomatoes), season to taste with salt and black pepper and stir in the caster (superfine) sugar and tomato purée (paste). Bring to the boil, then simmer, stirring occasionally, for 20 minutes.

3 Gently stir in the artichoke hearts and black olives and cook for 5 minutes.

4 Meanwhile, bring a large saucepan of lightly salted water to the boil. Add the spaghetti and the remaining oil and cook for 7–8 minutes, until tender but still firm to the bite.

5 Drain the spaghetti thoroughly and toss with the butter. Transfer the spaghetti to a large serving dish.

6 Pour the vegetable sauce over the spaghetti, garnish with the sprigs of fresh basil and serve immediately with olive bread.

Pasta & Bean Casserole

Serves 6

INGREDIENTS

225 g/8 oz/1¼ cups dried
    haricot (navy) beans,
    soaked overnight
    and drained
225 g/8 oz dried penne
6 tbsp olive oil
850 ml/1½ pints /3½ cups
    vegetable stock
2 large onions, sliced

2 garlic cloves, chopped
2 bay leaves
1 tsp dried oregano
1 tsp dried thyme
5 tbsp red wine
2 tbsp tomato purée (paste)
2 celery sticks (stalks), sliced
1 fennel bulb, sliced

115 g/4 oz/1⅝ cups sliced
    mushrooms
250 g/8 oz tomatoes, sliced
1 tsp dark muscovado sugar
4 tbsp dry white breadcrumbs
salt and pepper
salad leaves (greens) and
    crusty bread, to serve

1 Put the haricot (navy) beans in a large saucepan and add cold water to cover. Bring to the boil and boil vigorously for 20 minutes. Drain, set aside and keep warm.

2 Bring a large saucepan of lightly salted water to the boil. Add the penne and 1 tbsp of the olive oil and cook for about 3 minutes. Drain the pasta, set aside and keep warm.

3 Put the beans in a large, flameproof casserole. Add the vegetable stock and stir in the remaining olive oil, the onions, garlic, bay leaves, oregano, thyme, wine and tomato purée (paste). Bring to the boil, then cover and cook in a preheated oven at 180°C/350°F/Gas 4 for 2 hours.

4 Add the penne, celery, fennel, mushrooms

and tomatoes to the casserole and season to taste with salt and pepper. Stir in the muscovado sugar and sprinkle over the breadcrumbs. Cover the dish and cook in the oven for 1 further hour.

5 Serve hot with salad leaves (greens) and crusty bread.

Apricot Slices

Makes 12

INGREDIENTS

PASTRY:
225 g/8 oz/1³/4 cups
    wholemeal (whole wheat)
    flour
50 g/1³/4 oz finely ground
    mixed nuts

100 g/3¹/2 oz/¹/3 cup
    margarine, cut into small
    pieces
4 tbsp water
milk, to glaze

FILLING:
225 g/8 oz dried apricots
grated rind of 1 orange
300 ml/¹/2 pint/1¹/3 cups
    apple juice
1 tsp ground cinnamon
50 g/1³/4 oz/¹/3 cup raisins

1 Lightly grease a 23 cm/9 inch square cake tin (pan). To make the pastry (pie dough), place the flour and nuts in a mixing bowl and rub in the margarine with your fingers until the mixture resembles breadcrumbs. Stir in the water and bring together to form a dough. Wrap and leave to chill for 30 minutes.

2 To make the filling, place the apricots, orange rind and apple juice in a pan and bring to the boil. Simmer for 30 minutes until the apricots are mushy. Cool slightly, then blend to a purée. Stir in the cinnamon and raisins.

3 Divide the pastry (pie dough) in half, roll out one half and use to line the base of the tin. Spread the apricot purée over the top and brush the edges of the pastry (pie dough) with water. Roll out the rest of the dough to fit over the top of the apricot purée. Press down and seal the edges.

4 Prick the top of the pastry (pie dough) with a fork and brush with milk. Bake in a preheated oven, 200°C/ 400°F/Gas Mark 6, for 20–25 minutes until the pastry is golden. Leave to cool slightly before cutting into 12 bars. Serve warm.

Baked Tofu (Bean Curd) Cheesecake

Serves 6

INGREDIENTS

125 g/4 1/2 oz digestive
  biscuits (graham crackers),
  crushed
50 g/1 3/4 oz/10 tsp margarine,
  melted
50 g/1 3/4 oz stoned dates,
  chopped

4 tbsp lemon juice
rind of 1 lemon
3 tbsp water
350 g/12 oz or 2 x 285 g
  packets firm tofu (bean
  curd)

150 ml/1/4 pint/2/3 cup apple
  juice
1 banana, mashed
1 tsp vanilla flavouring
  (extract)
1 mango, peeled and chopped

1 Lightly grease an
18 cm/7 inch round
loose-bottomed cake
tin (pan).

2 Mix together the
digestive biscuit
(graham cracker) crumbs
and melted margarine in
a bowl. Press the mixture
into the base of the
prepared tin (pan).

3 Put the chopped dates,
lemon juice, rind and
water into a saucepan and
bring to the boil. Simmer

for 5 minutes until the
dates are soft, then mash
them roughly with a fork.

4 Place the mixture in a
blender or food
processor with the tofu
(bean curd), apple juice,
mashed banana and vanilla
flavouring (extract) and
process until the mixture is
a thick, smooth purée.

5 Pour the tofu (bean
curd) purée into the
prepared biscuit (cracker)
crumb base.

6 Bake in a preheated
oven, 180°C/350°F/
Gas Mark 4, for 30-40
minutes until lightly
golden. Leave to cool in
the tin (pan), then chill
thoroughly before serving.

7 Place the chopped
mango in a blender
and process until smooth.
Serve it as a sauce with the
chilled cheesecake.

Pineapple Upside-down Cake

Serves 6

INGREDIENTS

432 g/15 oz can unsweetened
  pineapple pieces, drained
  and juice reserved
4 tsp cornflour (cornstarch)
50 g/1³/4 oz/3 tbsp soft brown
  sugar
50 g/1³/4 oz/10 tsp margarine,
  cut into small pieces

125 ml/4 fl oz/¹/2 cup water
rind of 1 lemon

SPONGE:
50 ml/2 fl oz/¹/4 cup
  sunflower oil
75 g/2³/4 oz/¹/3 cup soft
  brown sugar
150 ml/¹/4 pint/²/3 cup water

150 g/5¹/2 oz/1¹/4 cups plain
  (all-purpose) flour
2 tsp baking powder
1 tsp ground cinnamon

1 Grease a deep 18 cm/7 inch cake tin (pan). Mix the reserved juice from the pineapple with the cornflour (cornstarch) until it forms a smooth paste. Put the paste in a saucepan with the sugar, margarine and water and stir over a low heat until the sugar has dissolved. Bring to the boil and simmer for 2-3 minutes until thickened. Leave to cool slightly.

2 To make the sponge, place the oil, sugar and water in a saucepan. Heat gently until the sugar has dissolved; do not allow it to boil. Set aside to cool. Sieve the flour, baking powder and cinnamon into a mixing bowl. Pour over the cooled sugar syrup and beat well to form a batter.

3 Place the pineapple pieces and lemon rind on the bottom of the tin (pan) and pour over 4 tablespoons of the pineapple syrup. Spoon the sponge batter on top.

4 Bake in a preheated oven, 180°C/350°F/Gas Mark 4, for 35-40 minutes until set and a fine metal skewer inserted into the centre comes out clean. Invert on to a plate, leave to stand for 5 minutes, then remove the tin (pan). Serve with the remaining syrup.

Date & Apricot Tart

Serves 6-8

INGREDIENTS

225 g/8 oz/1¾ cups plain wholemeal (whole wheat) flour
50 g/1¾ oz mixed nuts, ground
100 g/3½ oz/⅓ cup margarine, cut into small pieces

4 tbsp water
225 g/8 oz dried apricots, chopped
225 g/8 oz stoned dates, chopped
425 ml /¾ pint/2 cups apple juice

1 tsp ground cinnamon
grated rind of 1 lemon
custard, to serve (optional)

1 Place the flour and ground nuts in a bowl and rub in the margarine until the mixture resembles breadcrumbs. Stir in the water and bring together to form a dough. Wrap the dough and leave to chill for 30 minutes.

2 Meanwhile, place the apricots and dates in a saucepan with the apple juice, cinnamon and lemon rind. Bring to the boil, cover and simmer for 15 minutes until the fruit softens and can be mashed to a purée.

3 Reserve a small ball of pastry (pie dough) for making lattice strips. On a lightly floured surface, roll out the rest of the dough to form a round and use to line a 23 cm/9 inch loose-bottomed quiche tin (pan).

4 Spread the fruit filling over the base of the pastry (pie dough). Roll out the reserved pastry (pie dough) and cut into strips 1 cm/½ inch wide. Cut the strips to fit the tart and twist them across the top of the fruit to form a lattice pattern. Moisten the edges of the strips with water and seal them around the rim.

5 Bake in a preheated oven, 200°/400°F/Gas Mark 6, for 25-30 minutes until golden brown. Cut into slices and serve with custard, if using.

Fruit Crumble

Serves 6

INGREDIENTS

6 dessert pears,
1 tbsp stem (candied) ginger,
 chopped
1 tbsp molasses (dark
 muscovado sugar)
2 tbsp orange juice

TOPPING:
175 g/6 oz/1^1/$_2$ cups plain
 (all-purpose) flour
75 g/2^3/$_4$ oz/^{1}/$_3$ cup
 margarine, cut into small
 pieces

25 g/1 oz almonds, flaked
 (slivered)
25 g/1 oz/^{1}/$_3$ cup porridge
 oats
50 g/1^3/$_4$ oz molasses (dark
 muscovado sugar)

1 Lightly grease a
1 litre/2 pint/4^1/$_2$ cup
ovenproof dish.

2 Peel, core and quarter
the pears, then cut
them into slices. In a bowl,
mix together the pears,
ginger, molasses (dark
muscovado sugar) and
orange juice. Spoon
the mixture into the
prepared dish.

3 To make the crumble
topping, sieve (strain)
the flour into a mixing

bowl and rub in the
margarine with your fingers
until the mixture resembles
fine breadcrumbs. Stir in the
flaked (slivered) almonds,
porridge oats and molasses
(dark muscovado sugar)
and mix together well.

4 Sprinkle the crumble
topping evenly over the
pear and ginger mixture in
the dish.

5 Bake in a preheated
oven, 190°C/375°F/Gas
Mark 5, for 30 minutes

until the topping is golden
and the fruit tender. Serve.

VARIATION

*Stir 1 tsp ground mixed
spice (allspice) into the
crumble mixture in step 3
for added flavour,
if you prefer.*

Poached Allspice Pears

Serves 4

INGREDIENTS

4 large, ripe pears	2 tsp ground allspice	grated orange rind, to
300 ml/¹/₂ pint/1¹/₄ cups	60 g/2 oz/¹/₃ cup raisins	decorate
orange juice	2 tbsp light brown sugar	

1 Using an apple corer, core the pears. Using a sharp knife, peel the pears and cut them in half.

2 Place the pear halves in a large saucepan.

3 Add the orange juice, allspice, raisins and sugar to the pan and heat gently, stirring, until the sugar has dissolved. Bring the mixture to the boil for 1 minute.

4 Reduce the heat to low and leave to simmer for about 10 minutes, or until the pears are cooked,

but still fairly firm – test them by inserting the tip of a sharp knife.

5 Remove the pears from the pan with a slotted spoon and transfer to serving plates. Decorate and serve hot with the syrup.

VARIATION

Use cinnamon instead of the allspice and decorate with cinnamon sticks and fresh mint sprigs, if you prefer.

COOK'S TIP

The Chinese do not usually have desserts to finish off a meal, except at banquets and special occasions. Sweet dishes are usually served in between main meals as snacks, but fruit is refreshing at the end of a big meal.

Ginger Lychees with Orange Sorbet

Serves 4

INGREDIENTS

SORBET:
225 g/8 oz/1/4 cups caster
(superfine) sugar
450 ml/3/4 pint/2 cups cold
water
350 g/12 oz can mandarins, in
natural juice

2 tbsp lemon juice

STUFFED LYCHEES:
425 g/15 oz can lychees,
drained

60 g/2 oz stem (preserved)
ginger, drained and finely
chopped
lime zest, cut into diamond
shapes, to decorate

1 To make the sorbet, place the sugar and water in a saucepan and stir over a low heat until the sugar has dissolved. Bring the mixture to the boil and boil vigorously for 2-3 minutes.

2 Meanwhile, blend the mandarins in a food processor or blender until smooth. Press the blended mandarin mixture through a sieve until smooth. Stir the mandarin sauce into the syrup, together with the lemon juice. Set aside to cool.

3 Pour the mixture into a rigid, plastic container suitable for the freezer and freeze until set, stirring occasionally.

4 Meanwhile, drain the lychees on absorbent kitchen paper (paper towels).

5 Spoon the chopped ginger into the centre of the lychees.

6 Arrange the lychees on serving plates, garnish and serve with scoops of orange sorbet.

COOK'S TIP

It is best to leave the sorbet in the refrigerator for 10 minutes, so that it softens slightly, allowing you to scoop it to serve.

Eggless Sponge

Makes one 20 cm/8 inch cake

INGREDIENTS

225 g/8 oz/1¾ cups self-
raising wholemeal (self-
rising whole wheat) flour
2 tsp baking powder

175 g/6 oz/¾ cup caster
(superfine) sugar
6 tbsp sunflower oil
250 ml/9 fl oz/1 cup water

1 tsp vanilla flavouring
(extract)
4 tbsp strawberry or raspberry
reduced-sugar spread
caster (superfine) sugar, for
dusting

1 Grease two 20 cm/
8 inch sandwich cake
tins (layer pans) and line
them with baking
parchment.

2 Sieve (strain) the flour
and baking powder
into a large mixing bowl,
stirring in any bran
remaining in the sieve.
Stir in the caster
(superfine) sugar.

3 Pour in the sunflower
oil, water and vanilla
flavouring (extract) and
mix well for about

1 minute until the mixture
is a smooth consistency.

4 Divide the mixture
between the prepared
tins (pans).

5 Bake in a preheated
oven, 180°C/350°F/
Gas 4, for 25-30 minutes
until the centre springs
back when lightly touched.
Leave to cool in the tins
(pans), then turn out and
transfer to a wire rack.

6 To serve, remove the
baking parchment and

place one of the sponges
on to a serving plate.
Spread with the jam and
place the other sponge on
top. Dust with a little
caster (superfine) sugar.

VARIATION

*Use melted butter or
margarine instead of the
sunflower oil if you prefer,
but allow it to cool before
adding it to the dry
ingredients in step 3.*

This is a Parragon Book
First published in 2000
Parragon
Queen Street House
4 Queen Street
Bath BA1 1HE, UK

ISBN: 0-75253-373-8

Copyright © Parragon 2000

Printed in China

Note

Cup measurements in this book are for American cups. Tablespoons are assumed to be
15 ml. Unless otherwise stated, milk is assumed to be full fat, eggs are medium and
pepper is freshly ground black pepper.